T0065476

PLUG
INTO THE
POWER
OF
PRAYER

130 Prayer Points for Difficult Times

Evelyn Tolbert

WESTBOW
P R E S S®
A DIVISION OF THOMAS NELSON
& ZONDERVAN

WestBow Press books may be ordered through booksellers or by contacting:

WestBow Press
A Division of Thomas Nelson & Zondervan
1663 Liberty Drive
Bloomington, IN 47403
www.westbowpress.com
844-714-3454

All scriptures are taken from the New King James Version except where stated.

ISBN: 978-1-6642-6142-6 (sc)
ISBN: 978-1-6642-6143-3 (e)

Library of Congress Control Number: 2022905294

Print information available on the last page.

WestBow Press rev. date: 04/29/2022

CONTENTS

Acknowledgments vii

Introduction ix

1   Prayer of Restoration 1
2   Prayer against Scarcity 3
3   Prayer against Failure 5
4   Prayer against Anger and Bitterness 7
5   Prayer against Shame and Disgrace 9
6   Spoken Words 11
7   Financial Breakthrough 13
8   Prayers for Healing 15
9   Prayer for Preservation 17
10   Divine Favor 19
11   Prayer against Opposition 21
12   Entrapment and Protection 23
13   Disappointment and Discouragement 25
14   Prayer against the Spirit of Fear 27
15   Prayer for Abundance 29
16   Prayer against the Spirit of Unforgiveness 31
17   Hopelessness 33
18   Open Doors 35
19   Prayers against Evil Patterns 37
20   Additional Scripture-Based Prayers 39

ACKNOWLEDGMENTS

I want to thank all those who have been a source of support and encouragement. To my wonderful children and grandchildren, thank you for bringing joy to my life. I also want to thank my brothers and sister for their support. I love you all.

To the ones I call my sisters—Victoria Itebe, Edith Awofeso, Lynette Brown, and Elder Naomi Yeates—for encouraging and supporting me on this project, I say thank you.

INTRODUCTION

Prayer is one of the key elements of our walk with God. If you are not prayerful, you will be powerless before the enemy. You need prayers to survive in this challenging times. Prayer does not take away the troubles and challenges of life, but it does strengthen your spirit, man, and draws you closer to God. Jesus told us to pray always and not to lose heart. It is not advice—it is a command. As believers we need to find and make time for prayers every day.

> Then He spoke a parable to them, that men always ought to pray and not lose heart. (Luke 18:1)

1

PRAYER OF RESTORATION

So David inquire of the LORD saying, shall I pursue this troop? Shall I overtake them? And He answer him, "Pursue for you shall surely overtake them and without fail recover all. (1 Samuel 30:8)

When the Amalekites took David and his men's wives and children captive, and David inquired from God what to do. The LORD told David that everything taken will be restore back to him and he will recover all. (2 Samuel 9:7)

And I will restore to you the years that the swarming locust hath eaten, the crawling locust, the consuming locust, and the chewing locust. My great army which I sent among you.

You shall eat in plenty and be satisfied. And praise the name of the LORD your God Who has dealt wondrously with you; And My people shall never be put to shame. (Joel 2:25–26)

It is remarkable that the locusts not only destroyed the produce of that year but also ate up all the buds and barked trees so that they did not recover for years.

1.   O Lord, restore back to me every wasted years of my life, and let Your anointing for speed fall on me in the name of Jesus.

2.   O Lord, I shall recover everything the enemy has stolen from me in the name of Jesus.

3.   O Lord, restore to me the wasted years the locust has eaten in my destiny in the name of Jesus.

4.   O Lord, connect me with my destiny helpers who will help me achieve my divine purpose in the name of Jesus.

5.   Lord of abundance, let me flow in plenty, overflow, and multiply in the name of Jesus.

6.   I shall recover everything the enemy has stolen from me in the name of Jesus.

7.   O Lord, give me access where there is no access in the name of Jesus.

8.   O Lord, I take authority over all you have given me in the name of Jesus.

2

PRAYER AGAINST SCARCITY

And seven years of famine began to come, as Joseph had said. The famine was in all lands but in all the land of Egypt there was bread. (Genesis 41:54)

There I will provide for you, lest you and your household and all that you have, come to poverty, for there are still five years of famine. (Genesis 45:11)

9. O Lord, break the backbone of scarcity in my destiny in the name of Jesus.

10. Lord of abundance, let me dwell in abundance and overflow in the midst of scarcity in the name of Jesus.

Beloved, I pray that you may prosper in all things and be in health, just as your soul prosper. (3 John 1:2)

11. O Lord, expand my territory, enlarge my coast, and let me prosper spiritually and financially in the name of Jesus.

3

PRAYER AGAINST FAILURE

Life is full of ups and downs. There are challenges that we face that sometimes make us feel like a failure, be it a failure in marriage, business, education, or any aspect of our lives. We have a God who has given us the ability to succeed even when we feel we have failed.

> I can do all things through Christ that strengthens me. (Philippians 4:13)

> Cast your burden upon the LORD, and He shall sustain thee, He shall never suffer the righteous to be moved. (Psalm 55:22)

> My flesh and heart fail, But God is the strength of my heart, and my portion forever. (Psalm 73:26)

12. O Lord, give me the ability and power to do all things through Your strength and power for Your glory in the name of Jesus.

13. I cancel every spirit of failure and disappointment in my life in the name of Jesus.

14. O Lord, cancel every spirit of failure showing up at the point of my breakthrough in the name of Jesus.

15. Father, let the axe of God break every barrier, obstacle, and hindrance at the edge of my breakthrough in the name of Jesus.

16. O Lord, give me the strength to overcome every failure, weakness, and unpleasant situation in my life in Jesus's name.

17. O Lord, when my heart and flesh fail, give me Your divine strength in the name of Jesus.

18. O Lord, water every dry region in my life with your rivers of water in the name of Jesus.

19. O Lord, every power spending the night to pull me down be consumed by fire in the name of Jesus.

20. Every evil exchange against my destiny be nullified by Holy Ghost fire in the name of Jesus.

4

PRAYER AGAINST ANGER
AND BITTERNESS

Sometimes people or situations can make us angry. The Bible lets us know that we should not allow the spirit of anger to control us, nor should we be angry to the point it becomes a sin. In Psalm 37:8, the psalmist says that anger only causes harm, and we should cease from it.

> Let all bitterness, wrath, anger, clamor and evil speaking be put away from you, with all malice. And be kind to one another tenderhearted, forgiving one another even as God in Christ forgave you. (Ephesians 4:31–32)

> But I say to you that whoever is angry with his brother without a cause shall be in danger of the judgement and whoever says to his brother "Raca!" shall be in danger of the council, But whoever says, "You fool!" shall be in danger of hell fire. (Matthew 5:22)

> Do not hasten in your spirit to be angry, for anger rests in the bosom of fools. (Ecclesiastes 7:9)

21.   O Lord, take away all forms of bitterness and anger that dwell in me in the name of Jesus.

22.   O Lord, give me a heart of kindness and a spirit of forgiveness in the name of Jesus.

23. O Lord, remove from my heart the spirit of anger and renew a right spirit within me in the name of Jesus.

24. O Lord, give a forgiving heart to forgive those who have offended me in the name of Jesus.

If you have a spirit of anger that dwells in you, find out the root of it and resolve it, especially if you are always angry about minor things. Cast that spirit out of you because an angry spirit is not a good spirit for a believer.

5

PRAYER AGAINST SHAME
AND DISGRACE

To You, O Lord, I lift up my soul. O my God, I trust in You, let me not be ashamed, let not my enemy triumph over me. (Psalm 25:1–2)

Let them be ashamed who persecute me, but do not let me put to shame, Let them be dismayed. Bring on them the day of doom, and destroy them with double destruction. (Jeremiah 17:18)

25. 25. O Lord, tear off the garment of shame and disgrace from my destiny in the name of Jesus.

26. 26. O Lord, for my trouble, give me double portions of blessings in the name of Jesus.

27. 27. Lion of the tribe of Judah, let every spirit of shame around me be consumed by the fire of God in the name of Jesus.

28. 29. O Lord, put all my enemies to shame by making my life one of testimonies in the name of Jesus.

29. 30. O Lord, disconnect me from every deceiver and deceiving spirit in the name of Jesus.

5

PRAYER AGAINST SHAME AND DISGRACE

6

SPOKEN WORDS

Words are powerful. The words people say to you can hurt you, uplift you, or destroy you. People can curse you with the words that come out their mouths. We are not to speak evil or discouraging words to our fellow human beings.

> For the mouth of the wicked and the mouth of the deceitful; have opened against me. They have spoken against me with a lying tongue. They compassed me about also with words of hatred, and fought against me without a cause. (Psalm 109:2–3)

> So shall my word be that goes forth from my mouth; It shall not return to me void. But it shall accomplish what I please, and it shall prosper in the thing which I sent it. (Isaiah 55:11)

30.   31. O Lord, let every evil word spoken against my destiny be reversed to blessing by Holy Ghost fire in the name of Jesus.

31.   32. Let every evil meeting summoned against me be scattered by the fire of God in the name of Jesus.

32.   33. Let every tongue uttering curses or evil pronouncement into my destiny be silenced by Holy Ghost fire in the name of Jesus.

33.   34. O Lord, seal every loophole that enemies are using against my life by Holy Ghost fire in Jesus's name.

34.   35. O Lord, every one of Your spoken words regarding my life shall manifest in the name of Jesus.

35.   O Lord, let every evil speaker planted around me be disconnected from my life in the name of Jesus.

36.   O Lord, let every incantation and enchantment against my destiny be terminated in the name of Jesus.

7

FINANCIAL BREAKTHROUGH

God has promised us that He will meet us at the point of our need. In Matthew 6:25, Jesus said we should not worry about our lives, what we shall eat or drink, or the clothes we will wear. As humans, we are always worrying about not having enough for our daily needs. But God the provider will always provide for His children.

> But may the God of all grace, who called us to His eternal glory by Christ Jesus, after you have suffered a while, perfect, establish, strengthen and settle you. (1 Peter 5:10)

> But my God shall supply on your need according to his riches in glory. (Philippians 4:19)

37. O Lord, break every pattern of financial shame in my life in the name of Jesus.

38. I receive financial breakthrough with the power of the Holy Ghost in the name of Jesus.

39. Let every garment of poverty on me be burned by Holy Ghost fire in the name of Jesus.

40. I denounce every spirit of lack in my life in the name of Jesus. Let the anointing to excel and to succeed fall on me in the name of Jesus.

41. O Lord, strengthen me, establish and settle me by Your power in the name of Jesus.

Blessed be the God and Father of our Lord Jesus Christ, who hath blessed us with all spiritual blessings in heavenly places in Christ. (Ephesians 1:3)

42.   I receive every spiritual blessing from heaven in the name of Jesus.

8

PRAYERS FOR HEALING

Behold I will bring it health and healing: I will heal them and reveal to them abundance of peace and truth. (Jeremiah 35:6)

For I will restore health to you, and heal you of your wounds, says the Lord, because they called you an outcast saying, this is Zion no one seeks her. (Jeremiah 30:17)

Is anyone among you sick? Let them call the elders of the church to pray over them and anoint them with oil in the name of the Lord.

And the prayer of faith shall save the sick, and the Lord shall raise him up; and if he committed sins, they shall be forgiven. (James 5:14–15)

Heal me, Lord. And I shall be healed, save me and I shall be saved, for you are my praise. (Jeremiah 17:14)

43.   O Lord, heal me and I shall be healed, for you are the God of my praise in the name of Jesus.

44.   O Lord my healer, heal every one of my wounds in the name of Jesus.

45.   The Great Physician heal my soul, my body, and make me whole in the name of Jesus.

46. I decree and declare healing to every part of my body in the name of Jesus.

47. By the blood of Jesus, I flush out any strange element in my body in the name of Jesus.

48. O Lord, take away every illness in my body and restore unto me good health in the name of Jesus.

9

PRAYER FOR PRESERVATION

So shall they fear, The name of the Lord from the west, and His glory from the rising of the sun. When the enemy comes in like a flood. The spirit of the Lord will lift up a standard against him. (Isaiah 59:19)

The sun shall not strike you by day nor the moon by night.

The Lord shall preserve thee from all evil: He shall preserve thy soul.

The LORD shall preserve thy going out and thy coming in from this time forth, and even forever more. (Psalm 121:6–8)

Surely, He shall deliver you from the snare of the fowler, and from the perilous pestilence.

He shall cover you with His feathers and under His wings you shall take refuge.

His truth shall be your shield and buckler. (Psalm 91:3–4)

49. O Lord, raise a standard against enemies that rise up against me in the name of Jesus.

50. O Lord, let your wrath fall upon the evil plans of the enemy against my destiny in the name of Jesus.

51. O Lord, every power spending the night to pull me down or against my destiny be destroyed by Holy Ghost fire in the name of Jesus.

52. In the name of Jesus, every satanic power attacking my progress in the day or night be consumed by fire of God.

53. O Lord, deliver me from the plan of the wicked and surround me with your protective hand in the name of Jesus.

> Behold, a whirlwind of the LORD has gone forth in fury, a violent whirlwind. It will fall violently on the head of the wicked. (Jeremiah 23:19)

54. Lion of the tribe of Judah, let Your violent whirlwind of fire fall on the heads of my enemies in the name of Jesus.

55. O Lord, preserve me and my family in our coming and going in this life journey, we shall not die premature death in the name of Jesus.

56. O Lord, arise with your sword and break the arms of my enemies in the name of Jesus.

57. O Lord, put the hedge of protection around me and my family in the name of Jesus.

10

DIVINE FAVOR

Divine favor is when God gives you preference to others. Divine favor exalts the believer. Wisdom gives you favor of God.

A good man obtains favor from the LORD, but a man of wicked intentions He will condemn. (Proverbs 12 :2)

The king loved Esther more than the other women, and she obtained grace and favor in his sight more than all virgins, so he set the royal crown upon her head and made her queen instead of Vashti. (Esther 2:17)

Then the angel said to her, do not be afraid Mary, for you have found favor with God. (Luke 1:30)

58. O Lord, let me receive uncommon favor to excel in my destiny in the name of Jesus.

59. O Lord, I cancel every evil agenda against my divine favor in the name of Jesus.

60. Every power standing against the favor of God in my life be destroyed by Holy Ghost fire in the name of Jesus.

61. O Lord, open the doors of divine opportunity for me in the name of Jesus.

Therefore, your gates shall be open continually; They shall not be shut day or night, that men may bring to you the wealth of the gentiles, and their kings in procession. (Isaiah 60:11)

62.   O Lord of abundance, fill my cup with overflow and abundance in the name of Jesus.

63.   Every favor the Lord has for me shall not pass me by in the name of Jesus.

64.   O Lord wherever I go, I will stand out for favor and goodness in the name of Jesus.

11

PRAYER AGAINST OPPOSITION

Opposition is resistance from the enemy and persecution. You can face opposition because of your belief.

> Blessed are you when they revile and persecute you and say all kinds of evil against you for my sake. (Matthew 5:11)

> The adversaries of the Lord shall be broken in pieces, from heaven He will thunder against them. The Lord will judge the ends of the earth. (1 Samuel 2:10)

> Remember me, my God, for good according to all that I have done for this people. (Nehemiah 5:19)

> What then shall we say to these things? If God is for us who can be against us? (Romans 8:31)

65. O Lord, any opposition or mountain standing in the way of my progress be removed by Holy Ghost fire in the name of Jesus.

66. O Lord, open the book of remembrance and remember me. Let my good deeds speak for me in the name of Jesus.

67. O Lord, let the enemies that have walked over me drink the cup of Your fury in the name of Jesus.

68. Every mountain and obstacles not allowing me to achieve my goals in life be destroyed by fire of God in the name of Jesus.

69. Every stronghold of darkness pulling me down and setting me backward be terminated by Holy Ghost fire in the name of Jesus.

12

ENTRAPMENT AND PROTECTION

Entrapment is the act of tricking someone to do what they will not normally do. You can be threatened or intimidated. The Pharisees and scribes tried several times to entrap Jesus in so many ways.

> So they watched Him, and sent spies who pretended to be righteous that they might seize on His words to deliver Him to the power and the authority of the governor. (Luke 20:20)

> Behold, the wicked brings forth iniquity; Yes, he conceives trouble and brings forth falsehood.

> He made a pit and dug it out, and has fallen into the ditch which he made.

> His trouble shall return upon his head, and his violent dealing shall come down on his crown. (Psalm 7:14–16)

70. O Lord, let my enemies fall into every trap they have set for me in the name of Jesus.

71. O Lord, let the evil wishes of my enemies return back to them by fire in the name of Jesus.

72. O Lord, let my enemies rise against themselves in the name of Jesus.

> There they are in great fear, where no fear was, For God has scattered the bones of him who encamps against

you. You have put them to shame, because God has despised them. (Psalm 53:5)

73. O Lord, scatter the bones of those who encamp against me in the name of Jesus.

74. O Lord, let Your fire consume every soul hunter of my life in the name of Jesus.

75. O Lord, let Your rock of offense and wrath of anger overtake all my enemies in the name of Jesus.

Seeing it is a righteous thing with God to repay tribulation to those who trouble you. (2 Thessalonians 1:3)

76. O Lord, bring me out of the grave the enemy had dug for me and let my enemy fall into that grave in the name of Jesus.

77. O Lord, trouble those that trouble me and repay them with tribulation in the name of Jesus.

Deliver me from my enemies, O my God, defend me from those who rise up against me.

Deliver me from the workers of iniquity; and save me from blood thirsty men. (Psalm 59:1–2)

78. O Lord, disappoint the expectation of my enemies and those waiting for me to cry in the name of Jesus.

79. O Lord, defend me from those who rise against me and save me from blood thirsty men in the name of Jesus.

And the Lord shall deliver me from every evil work and will preserve me unto His heavenly kingdom: to Him be glory forever and ever. Amen. (2 Timothy 4:18)

80. O Lord, the deliverer, deliver me and my family from every evil work of the enemy and preserve our lives in Jesus's name.

13

DISAPPOINTMENT AND DISCOURAGEMENT

Life is full of disappointments. You can be disappointed by people, friends, or families. God is the only one that does not disappoint man. He gives you courage in the midst of your disappointment if you put your trust in Him.

> He heals the broken hearted, and binds up their wounds. (Psalm 147:3)

> The Lord is good, a stronghold in the day of trouble. And He knows those who trust in Him. (Nahum 1:7)

> And let us not grow weary while doing good, for in due season we shall reap if we do not lose heart. (Galatians 6:9)

81. Every garment of disappointment that I am wearing be consumed by fire in the name of Jesus.

82. O Lord, every spirit of disappointment in my destiny be destroyed by Holy Ghost fire in the name of Jesus.

83. O Lord, let the spirit of discouragement be removed from my destiny in the name of Jesus.

84. O Lord, give me strength when I am weary and courage when I am faced with disappointment in the name of Jesus.

85. O Lord, I terminate the spirit of disappointment and discouragement in my destiny in the name of Jesus.

86. Any power-sponsoring affliction in my life be consumed by fire in the name of Jesus.

87. Every pattern of disappointment operating in my life be canceled and replaced with the goodness of the Lord in the name of Jesus.

14

PRAYER AGAINST THE SPIRIT OF FEAR

To fear is to be afraid of something, to have anxiety, to be terrified or feel apprehension of impending evil. In Matthew 25: 25, it was fear that made the servant with one talent bury his talent. He said he was afraid, and went and hid the talent in the ground.

> For God has not given us the spirit of fear, but of power and of love and a sound mind. (2 Timothy 1:7)

> For I, the Lord your God, I will hold your right hand, saying to you, "Fear not, I will help you." (Isaiah 41:13)

> So that we may boldly say, The Lord is my helper, and I will not fear what man shall do to me. (Hebrews 13:6)

88.   O Lord, I reject every spirit of fear that dwells within me; I receive the spirit of love and sound mind in the name of Jesus.

89.   O Lord, help me to trust you and cast my burden on you in the name of Jesus.

90.   O Lord, strengthen my faith in you, and take away the spirit of fear in me in Jesus's name.

91.   Every power that is putting fear in my life be consumed by Holy Ghost fire in the name of Jesus.

92.   Every stronghold of fear in my life be consumed by fire in the name of Jesus.

93. O Lord, I bind and cast out the spirit of fear that is preventing me from succeeding in life in the name of Jesus.

    The Lord is my light and my salvation; whom shall I fear? The Lord is the strength of my life, of whom shall I be afraid? (Psalm 27:1)

94. O Lord, I put my confidence in You, in Your truth, wisdom, and promises in the name of Jesus.

95. O Lord, give me strength in the midst of adversity; remove the spirit of fear from my life and strengthen my faith in You in the name of Jesus.

PRAYER FOR ABUNDANCE

Abundance is having more than enough of anything, having surplus and overflow—having a substantial amount of something. It could be material or spiritual, but you need both to live a life of abundance.

> Now to Him who is able to do exceedingly abundantly above all that we ask or think, according to the power that works in us. (Ephesians 3:20)

> And God is able to make all grace abound toward you, that you, always having all sufficiency in all things, may have an abundance for every good work. (2 Corinthians 9:8)

> Beloved, I pray that you may prosper in all things and be in health, just as your soul prospers. (3 John 1:2)

> And my God shall supply all your needs according to His riches in glory by Christ Jesus. (Philippians 4:19)

96. In the name of Jesus, I declare and decree that I will live and walk in abundance.

97. The Lord is my shepherd, and I shall not lack or be of want anymore in my destiny in the name of Jesus.

98. The Lord of provision shall supply all my needs according to His riches in glory in the name of Jesus.

99. In the name of Jesus, I shall prosper in all that I do and will be a financial pillar of the kingdom of God.

100. I declare and decree that I will continually dwell in overflow and abundance in the name of Jesus.

16

PRAYER AGAINST THE SPIRIT OF UNFORGIVENESS

Forgiveness is not an easy thing to do. It is something most of us struggle with. You will be offended, betrayed, or hurt by people, but you have to find it in your heart to forgive them.

Jesus forgave those who crucified Him. He said, "Father, forgive them for they know not what they do" (Luke 23:24). Forgiveness is not for the person who offends you, but for you. An unforgiving spirit can hinder your prayers.

> For if you forgive men their trespasses, your heavenly Father will also forgive you.
>
> But if you do not forgive men their trespasses, neither will your Father forgive your trespasses. (Matthew 6:14–15)
>
> Then Peter came to Him and said, "Lord, how often shall my brother sin against me. And forgive him? Up to seven times?"
>
> Jesus said to him, I do not say to you, up to seven times, but up to seventy times seven. (Matthew 18:21–22)
>
> And whenever you stand praying, if you have anything against anyone, forgive him, that your Father in heaven may also forgive you your trespasses. (Mark 11:25)

101. O Lord, help me to have a forgiving heart; give me the ability to forgive those that have offended or hurt me in the name of Jesus. O Lord, any spirit of resentment, hatred, or unforgiveness in me be removed by Holy Ghost fire in the name of Jesus.

102. O Lord, take away the spirit of anger, bitterness, and stubbornness in my life and renew a right spirit within me in the name of Jesus.

O Lord, give the grace to forgive all those that have offended and wronged me in the name of Jesus.

103. O Lord, I forgive all those that have hurt me, and I release the past and the spirit of unforgiveness in the name of Jesus.

HOPELESSNESS

When all hope is lost and everything seems hopeless and impossible, look unto Jesus, the author and finisher of our faith. Let God help you, and let Him bring joy back into your life. He gives us hope when all hope is lost.

> But for him who is joined to all the living there is hope, for a living dog is better than a dead lion. (Ecclesiastes 9:4)

> May the God of hope fill you with all joy and peace in believing, that you may abound in hope by the power of the Holy Spirit. (Romans 15:13)

> Uphold me according to Your word, that I may live; And do not let me be ashamed of my hope. (Psalm 119:116)

104. O Lord, I bring unto you every burden that am carrying, and I lay them before You in the name of Jesus.

105. O Lord, heal my broken heart and spirit; give me hope when everything looks hopeless in the name of Jesus.

106. O Lord, give me the grace to wait on You, and give me strength in my waiting in the name of Jesus.

107. O Lord, let Your joy dwell in me; let me remember that I am loved by You in my circumstances in the name of Jesus.

108. My hope is You, O Lord; do not let me be ashamed, and let Your peace and joy continually dwell within me in the name of Jesus.

18

OPEN DOORS

We all need doors of opportunity to be open for us, but not every door that opens is a door of opportunity. Sometimes a door will open that looks like a door of divine opportunity, but it can be a door of failure or disappointment. You need a discerning spirit to know what kind of door is opened for you.

> Suddenly there was a great earthquake, so that the foundations of the prison were shaken and immediately all the doors were opened and everyone's chains were loosed. (Acts 16:26)

109. O Lord, open for me the doors of divine opportunity, blessings, and favor for me in the name of Jesus.

110. O Lord, uproot and destroy every foundational problem affecting my life in the name of Jesus.

> Therefore, your gates shall be open continually. They shall not be shut day or night, that men may bring to you the wealth of the Gentiles, and their kings in procession. (Isaiah 60:11)

111. I decree and declare the gate of blessings in my destiny to remain open continually in the name of Jesus.

112. All evil gates standing against my family destiny be shut by Holy Ghost fire in the name of Jesus.

They obey and serve Him. They shall spend their days in prosperity and their years in pleasure. (Job 36:11)

113. O Lord, let Your light and glory shine upon my life and upon my family in Jesus's name.

114. O Lord, give me grace to be in obedient to Your word, let me spend my days in prosperity and years in pleasure in the name of Jesus.

For a great and effective door has opened to me, and there are many adversaries. (1 Corinthians 16:9)

115. O Lord, I pray that all the doors of opportunity the enemy has closed in my destiny be opened in the name of Jesus.

116. O Lord, enemies will not close the door of my divine opportunity and blessings that you have opened for me in the name of Jesus.

19

PRAYERS AGAINST EVIL PATTERNS

An evil pattern is the repetition of a negative occurrence in one's personal life. Some are passed on from generation to generation. Evil patterns are not mere coincidences. You need to recognize the evil pattern in your life to be able to break it. In some families, the pattern is sudden death at a certain age; for others, it is divorce. Sometimes there is a pattern of being barren or not finding a marriage. Recognize which pattern exists in your family, and pray for it to be broken.

Sarah was barren until she was ninety years old, and Isaac's wife Rebekah was barren until Isaac interceded for her. Jacob's second wife Rachel was barren until God remembered Rachel. This is not coincidence—these are patterns.

> Now Isaac pleaded with the Lord for his wife, because she was barren; and the Lord granted his plea, and Rebekah his wife conceived. (Genesis 25:21)

> When the Lord saw that Leah was unloved, He opened her womb; but Rachel was barren. (Genesis 29:31)

117. O Lord, arise and destroy every evil pattern in my family in the name of Jesus.

118. Every pattern of sudden death operating in my family be canceled in the name of Jesus

119. Every demonic chain tying my family down be broken by Holy Ghost fire in the name of Jesus.

120. O Lord, every pattern of barrenness existing in my blood line be canceled in the name of Jesus.

121. I decree and declare every forces of darkness operating against my family destiny be terminated by Holy Ghost fire.

122. O Lord, every pattern of affliction operating in my life and family be broken by the fire of God in Jesus name.

123. Every pattern of failure existing in my family be canceled by Holy Ghost fire in the name of Jesus.

124. I reject every spirit of lack, poverty, premature death, failure, and barrenness in my family in the name of Jesus.

125. O Lord, the anointing to excel, the anointing for speed, let it fall on me and my family in the name of Jesus.

126. Everyone in my life that is assigned to destroy or alter my destiny, Lord, terminate their assignment in the name of Jesus.

127. O Lord, every reoccurring problem in my life be canceled in the name of Jesus.

128. Let every plan, plot, or agenda of the enemy against my destiny be canceled by Holy Ghost fire.

129. O Lord, terminate and cancel the agenda of the enemy against my destiny in the name of Jesus.

20

ADDITIONAL SCRIPTURE-BASED PRAYERS

Give them, O Lord, what will You give? Give them a miscarrying womb and dry breasts.

Lord, give my enemies a miscarrying womb and dry breast in their evil plot against me in the name of Jesus. (Hosea 9:14)

Deliver me from the sword, my precious life from the power of dog.

In the name of Jesus, I declare and decree deliverance from the power of dog in the name of Jesus. (Psalm 22:20)

But against none of the children of Israel shall a dog move its tongue, against man or beast, that you may know that the Lord does make a different between the Egyptians and Israel. (Exodus 11:7)

O Lord, silence any dog barking against my destiny in the name of Jesus.

But He answered and said, "Every plant which My heavenly father has not planted will be uprooted. (Matthew 15:13)

O Lord, uproot everything that You did not plant in my life and destiny by Holy Ghost fire in the name of Jesus.

> I will punish Bel in Babylon, and I will bring out of his mouth what he has swallowed, and the nations shall not stream to him anymore. Yes, the wall of Babylon shall fall.
>
> I decree and declare that whatever belongs to me that the earth has swallowed up be vomited in the name of Jesus. (Jeremiah 51:44)

> Therefore thus says the Lord God "Surely I am against Pharaoh King of Egypt and will break his arms, both strong one and the one that was broken; and I will make the sword fall out of his hand. (Ezekiel 30:22)

O Lord, break the arms of every pharaoh that is against my life and destiny in the name of Jesus.

> Then Elisha said, "Hear the word of the LORD. Thus says the Lord 'Tomorrow about this time a seah of fine flour shall be sold for a shekel and two seahs of barley for a shekel at the gate of Samaria.'" (2 Kings 7:1)

O Lord, let my tomorrow be better than today; let no evil befall me in the name of Jesus.

> Thus says the LORD to His anointed, To Cyrus, whose right hand I have held, To subdue nations before him, And loose the armor of Kings, To open before him the double doors, so that gates will not be shut. (Isaiah 45:1)

O Lord, let the divine gates and doors of my destiny continually remain open for me in the name of Jesus.
O Lord, close all evil gates that are open before me in the name of Jesus.

O Lord, all evil gates, controlling powers manipulating my life and my family, be consumed by fire in the name of Jesus.

In the name of Jesus, every evil covenant, agreement standing against my destiny, be destroyed by Holy Ghost fire in the name of Jesus.

> Having wiped out the handwriting of requirements that was against us, which was contrary to us. And He has taken it out of the way having nailed it to the cross. (Colossians 2:14)

Every evil word written against my life and my family be erased by the fire of God in the name of Jesus.

All handwriting against my destiny be erased by Holy Ghost eraser in the name of Jesus.

> For the weapons of our warfare are not carnal but mighty through God to the pulling of strongholds. (2 Corinthians 10:4)

O Lord, send your fire to consume all evil altars created against me or my family in the name of Jesus.

Every stronghold of darkness against my destiny shall be pulled down by fire of God in the name of Jesus.

In the name of Jesus, I tear down the altars of delay, poverty, and failure in my life in the name of Jesus.

> There I will make the horn of David grow, I will prepare a lamp for My anointed. His enemies I will cloth with shame, but upon himself his crown shall flourish. (Psalm 133:17–18)

O Lord, clothe my enemies with the garment of shame and disgrace in the name of Jesus.

> There are, it may be so many language in the world, and none of them is without significance. (1 Corinthians 14:10)

Any voice of failure speaking against my life be consumed by fire of God in the name of Jesus.

> For thus says the LORD GOD; Bring up an assembly against them, give them up to trouble and plunder. Ezekiel 23:46

O Lord, let all my enemies be troubled and plundered by their enemies in the name of Jesus.

> Again, a new commandment I write to you which thing is true in Him and you, because the darkness is passing away and true light is already shinning. (1 John 2:8)

O Lord, let your light shine upon my life and destiny in the name of Jesus.

> Thus says the LORD GOD, "It shall not stand, Nor shall it come to pass." (Isaiah 7:7)

In the name of Jesus, the devious plan of the enemy against my life and destiny shall not come to stand or come to pass in the name of Jesus.

> Take counsel together, but it will come to nothing, speak word it will not stand, for God is with us. (Isaiah 8:10)

In the name of Jesus, the expectation of the enemy against me shall not come to manifestation in the name of Jesus.

Every gate of evil working against me be dismantled and broken in the name of Jesus.

> But those who wait on the LORD, shall renew their strength. They shall mount up with wings like eagles. They shall run and not be weary. They shall walk and not faint. (Isaiah 40:31)

O Lord, strengthen me in my waiting and weakness in the name of Jesus.

> I will make them and the places all around My hill
> a blessing, and I will cause showers to come in their
> season, there shall be showers of blessing. (Ezekiel 34:26)

O Lord of provision, God of increase, shower me with Your blessings in every area of my life in the name of Jesus.

O Lord, create an access for me where there is no access to divine opportunities, favor, and blessings in the name of Jesus.

> Plead my cause, O Lord, with those who strive with me,
> Fight against those who fight against me. (Psalm 35:1)

O Lord, contend against those who contend against me, and fight every of my battle in name of Jesus.

> Let those be put to shame and brought to dishonor, who
> seek after my life, let those be turned back and brought
> to confusion who plot my hurt. (Psalm 35:4)

In the name of Jesus, bring shame and dishonor to the enemies after my life, and let them be put to confusion.

> Since it is a righteous thing with God to repay with
> tribulation those who trouble you. (1 Thessalonians 1:6)

O Lord repay those that trouble me with tribulation in the name of Jesus.

> In righteousness you shall be established, You shall be
> far from oppression, for you shall not fear; And from
> terror, for it shall not come near you. (Isaiah 54:14)

O Lord, establish me in Your righteousness and destroy the plans of the oppressors in the name of Jesus.

As you pray these prayers, you can do praise and worship before each prayer session. Ask the Holy Spirit to minister to you, and the God that answer prayers will answer your prayers.

My Journey To Becoming A Registered Nurse

My Destination To My Career Choice

My Journey To
Becoming A Registered Nurse

My Destination To My
Career Choice

Joyce V. Morgan

ISBN: Softcover   978-1-6641-6185-6
               eBook   978-1-6641-6184-9

Print information available on the last page.

Rev. date: 03/11/2021

To order additional copies of this book, contact:
Xlibris
844-714-8691
www.Xlibris.com
Orders@Xlibris.com
824226

Contents

Nurses.. 1

This is my journey.. 3

The function of education is to think intensively and to think critically. Intelligence plus character- that is the goal of true education.

—Dr. Martin Luther King Jr.

Nothing in the world is more dangerous that sincere ignorance and conscientious stupidity.

—Dr. Martin Luther King Jr.

I refused to let anyone make me become less
than my capability of being. Only God and
I alone are the judge of that decision.

—Joyce V. Morgan

In God I trust.

MY JOURNEY TO BECOMING

A REGISTERED NURSE

I was 16 years old on this photo.

Nurses

WHO ARE THEY?

I would like to speak to the question.

Nurses are your front line of defense in the health-care system.

We burn a candle for you twenty-four hours, seven days a week (just for you).

We are your caretakers.

We are your advocates.

We nurture, for that is our nature.

We were especially selected to care for you, by the best of those who have gone before us.

We are the cream of the crop; therefore, it is our privilege to care for you.

We keep you informed of your rights when you are most vulnerable.

Nurses ensure that you are receiving the gold standard of care because it is your birthright.

Most of all, we truly care, and when you become better and win your plight, we rejoice in your delight that you will be able to pursue a healthy life.

By Joyce V. Morgan, RN, PHN, WHNP, MSN, FNP

This is my journey

I first knew I wanted to become a nurse when I was four years old. Being that I was a sickly child as I was an allergy-asthmatic, with multiple clinic visits three times a week, I found my purpose.

That purpose turned me into a nurse. The conclusion came to me after each visit as I always felt better after my treatments. The only conclusion that came to me was that I wanted to be one of those people who made other people feel better, coupled with the realization that I was orphaned at thirteen months of age and on my second foster home during that time.

Now my first realization of a home that I thought was real, I may have been five years old. I had attended kindergarten already.

At the age of six years old, I was told that I had no real mother by the only mother I had ever known. My first foster mother told me this when they came to remove us from the foster home due to domestic violence. It was a beautiful spring day, and I can remember very clear and sunny skies. I remember holding on to my foster mother; her name was Ruby. I was holding her so tight with all my tiny strength and was screaming and crying to the top of my soul. The social worker was trying to pull us apart. My sister was sitting at the back seat of the social worker's county car. She was oblivious as to what was going on. The only way I let go was when my mother bent down and said softly in my ear, "I am not your real mother, Joyce."

I immediately released her as I thought that I would go to jail if I didn't. I looked up at her, and we were both crying. That was the first time I had to suck it up. After all, I had a sister to take care of. While I sit here editing my thoughts and tears rolling down my cheeks, I walked to the front door to turn the porch light on. It came to me, or the Holy Spirit said, "Stop. I told you, 'Thou shall not want.'" We left the second home after getting all acclimated to their way of life after three years due to economizing in foster children.

Now I know you are wondering why we were removed from the third foster home after five years. Well, I told my older brother who was twenty-one years old, "Thank God." He was home on leave from the army. I explained to him what was going on in that home. I was thirteen years old at the time. My brother and I had a plan to do a surprise sting. These crimes were mental, physical, and sexual abuse, which had been going on for years. I won't elaborate because it is too painful. I know people love juicy details. I do believe that I was one of the fortunate ones to move on and get on with my life.

I was in charge of whom I became or who I was to become. I was determined that as long as I was alive and in my right frame of mind, I would make chicken shit into chicken soup. I was embraced by the Holy Spirit and asked God to lead me on the good path that I had chosen for myself. Most of my orphan family didn't make it. They live in and through me.

My daily prayer is to ask "God to give me the courage to do what I have to do and the strength to do what I think I can't do. Undeniably how I know my faith in God Almighty will carry me through all the rest." We put a stop to crimes that were taking place in that home. The day of removal, the social worker made an impromptu visit, and we were told again to get in that country car.

I knew what was happening, but the other two girls did not. Soon off we went. When we arrived at the orphan home after dinner, we were served leftovers from what had been cooked earlier for dinner. Guess what it was? Beans. We ate beans three days a week in that damn foster home. That was the last thing I wanted.

I spent two separate incarcerations of seven months each in the orphan home (jail sentences). Placement was temporary until they could find us a home. I had school every day, amen. I was glad because I wanted to be a nurse. We had grades 7–12 in one classroom; that was all we had. I even remember the teacher's name. We called her Ms. Sharon. She was twenty-four years old. She was kind and tolerant. Most of the children were troublesome, disruptive, and distracting.

Speaking of jail, the orphanage home was called Sneadergers Cottage. That was the name of the orphanage that is located off 150th Avenue in San Leandro, California. The location was right next door to the juvenile hall, which is slightly up the hill. I once had to make a trip up the hill for twenty-four-hour isolation for getting into a fight. The experience helped me make some quick alterations to my future, believe me. I did my time. I had plenty of time to think and plan my options in life.

My first fight. I tell you that made me never want to go to the big house as an adult. I was too short to see out of the steel door window. I tried jumping up to try to see what was going on. Looking back, I know that made the situation sequestered confinement.

The breakfast served was cold. I was served cold oatmeal, cold toast, and milk. Lunch was gangrene lunch meat and hard white bread with warm milk. The dinner was cold beans, corn bread, with lukewarm milk. When time came for my release from my jail cell, they unlocked the door, and I was set free. I walked down the hill accompanied by my favorite counselor to resume whatever activities that were going on at the time.

One thing about my stay in juvie was that it was the longest twenty-four hours in my life. That was a cool-off reflection time for me. That soap, wow. After I woke up that morning and washed my face, using a white bar soap, I smiled when I saw my friends. That first smile, I thought my face was going to crack open. I definitely can say there was no moisturizer in it, looking back. I don't know what that bar of soap was made of. I was told it was made from horse fat. One sad thing about being in an orphan home was we only got one visitor between both stays. My older brother was five years older than myself.

The orphan children got one hour for visitations on Saturdays. I remember the question I asked my brother when visiting hours were over was if he could bring us some chips the next time. But he never came back again. We were told that he had joined the US Army service. My biological grandmother lived in Hayward, California. Can you believe she never made a social call or came to visit us? May her rotten soul live in the underworld. In spite of that devil, my siblings and I made it in spite of her.

None of us went to jail or found ourselves on drugs and accusing the system. What we attributed it to among ourselves was that we knew not to get in trouble because we had no one to call to help us. When you get that first phone call, no parents, no lawyer, no relatives that we knew of or who knew us. Now I have always had a job for as long as I can remember, starting as early as twelve years old (child labor with no pay). This was where I taught myself my work ethic. This was in that third foster home that we were removed from that landed us in the orphan home in the first place. I try to be the best at whatever I did. I will let you in on what it was that I had to accomplish.

I spent my summers and weekends working in the kitchen of my foster mother's SNIF home doing the work of two grown women so she wouldn't have to pay out the salary.

My assignment was to wash all the dishes, set up the meal trays, and put the right names in order of room and bed numbers. Now this was when I learned what a low-salt (Na) diet, diabetic diet, and puree diet consist of. I even swept and mopped the floor twice a day. That mop weighed more than I did. I always helped pass the trays and sometimes fed the patients. Remember I was twelve years old.

Now here we were 1968. I was transferred to a school where I had heard you could start your nursing classes; this was tenth grade, mind you. The school was named Grant High in Oakland, California. It was a continuation school. Now what I discovered was that it was a poorly designed course to lead you to a dead-end job of what is known today as an NA without the C. After realizing this is not what I thought it would be, I finished out the year and transferred back to a high school that I knew was totally accredited: Oakland Technical High School. I thought I was getting ahead. I was always thinking and planning. That is just the way my brain works. I don't wait until my back is up against the wall to start thinking about my immediate circumstances. I eventually graduated, with real options to fulfill my nursing dreams.

I graduated from my accredited high school in 1971. I was feeling very accomplished and on my way. The most profound event at the ceremony was the song that was chosen. It was "Bridge over Troubled Waters." As I sat there, I was thinking of my troubled waters. In the order of occurrences, once I graduated, I was already a mother with one child and one two months on the way walking across the stage. I was thinking I had to find another job because I would no longer have my work-study job through the public school system. My work-study job was at Highland Hospital as a candy stripper.

This was another sign that I knew I was destined to be a nurse. I saw many procedures and surgeries; it actually prepared me for nursing School. So after graduation from high school, there was no time to celebrate; I had to work. My studio apartment rent was eighty-eight dollars a month. I immediately enrolled in junior college to get my prenursing courses for nursing school. I was shooting for my BSN.

Surprise, surprise. As I had completed my ninety units, I thought I had completed on time, along with the fact that I was in the counselor's office every month. The class that was missing was anthropology taught by an instructor named Joan King.

The class was reported that I had never taken the course; I had received a grade of B. We were shown our grade so we knew what grade was to be awarded and was to be granted to us. That was so sad. I couldn't fight it, and I enjoyed the class very much. Now of course, she, the instructor, was no longer on staff and nowhere to be located by me. Hold on. I was told that I was three units short and will not be able to graduate.

I and my then husband were excited that we were going to graduate at the same time from different schools, in the same year. I was attending the old Merritt Junior College, and he was attending the new Merritt Junior College. We had grants, student loans, meal tickets, and free child care that were provided by the college. We split up to gain more income. We also had work-study jobs, and we were able to buy a new car off the dealer floor with work study jobs.

We bought a 1974 Javelin automobile. Can you believe we bought it with work-study jobs? I tell you I was working it Bam! So one of us graduated. I must say it set me back. I started Laney Junior College in 1974 after working at McDonald's for a year. I had been taking the LVN entrance exam, but I never made the cut.

One day while I was working, I decided to walk over to the tower at Laney Junior College; that was what it was called. I spoke to the director of the program. I went into her office after being invited in, of course, and told her why I was there. She explained to me that every year, they were elevating the passing score because people weren't doing well with the previous scores. I said to her, "Well what am I to tell my grandchildren? That I failed?" When I was never even given the opportunity to try, I was thinking students must have been passing this program because it is still being funded, or it wasn't diversified enough in the program now that I am looking back. She looked at me and said, "I was always right under the elevation to increasing the scores."

Hold on. I will never forget what she decided to do. She told me, the director, "I want you to write every word you can think of that start with an *S* and *T*." She gave me a pencil and a sheet of paper, then she timed me with a stopwatch. When I finished, she said, "You will start the program in February 1974." I completed the program on time in 1976. I did end up receiving an associate's degree with my LVN and an associate's degree in social science. Mission accomplished. Now I know you may be wondering what happened to that BSN. Well, I will let you in on that fiasco. Before I graduated from high school, I had applied to every nursing school that I could get to on the AC transit bus system.

Merritt College Associate Degree
Nursing Program
cordially invites you to attend a

Pinning Ceremony

for

Graduate Nurses

on Friday evening, June 10, 1983

at 7:00 p.m.

The ceremony will be celebrated

in the Auditorium at

Highland Hospital

Oakland, California

Following the ceremony there will

be a reception

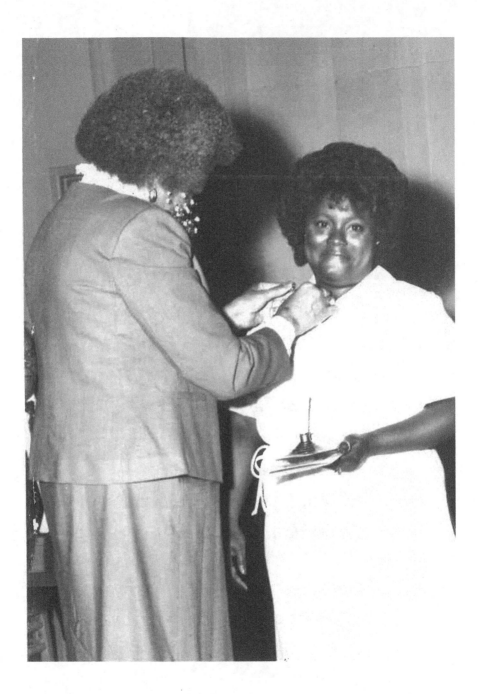

Registered Nurse Graduation at Highland
Hospital Auditorium, Oakland California

Although my heart was set on BSN, Merritt Junior College program was close to my neighborhood, and I would be in school while my children were in school and my then husband would be at work. I know that choice wasn't a BSN program, but it was my best option to open the door. I can't tell you when I saw my first black RN. I often would take the bus up to 25000 Campus Drive to Merritt Junior College to check on my placement on the list. I spoke with the same director of the program each time. I won't use her name, but my last meeting with her, she told me that at 135 pounds, I was too fat. I remember I hadn't started the LVN program yet, but the LVN program was the first door that opened. I always had more than one rabbit in the hat.

I can tell you I had the sense enough to go through the first door that opened. That's my motto. Now this means when they slam the front door in your face, I go to the back door, I go through the window, or I come down the chimney. Bottom line—never give up. I worked as an LVN for about four years mostly through the registry. I didn't want to deal with the politics. It was around this time I started thinking about buying a home.

In 1979, I applied to Alameda County. I got a letter for an interview and scored a verbal 98 percent. I made number 2 on the list. I can still remember who interviewed me: a white male named Bob Reed, head nurse, and a black female, Cathy Kittle, a Highland Hospital diploma graduate nurse. They both knew me well as an excellent LVN through the nurse's registry. I remember the question that I missed in that interview. It was, What is the most important assessment on a patient? The answer was level of consciousness (LOC).

I started my first nursing job on October 27, 1980, at Central Health Clinic located in Oakland, California. Oh, what a proud day. The position was in pediatrics, my least favorite area. I did learn to love it. I had good hours—8:00 a.m. to 5:00 p.m.—with weekends and holidays off. Moving up in the world, or so I thought. My dream came to visit me again. I had heard that Highland Hospital has started an RN one-year upgrade program. I immediately called the director of nurses at Highland Hospital. Well within a year after monthly phone calls, sometimes weekly and daily, being unwavering about my mission. I was in. Here and now in 1981 at twenty-eight years old, so proud of myself sitting in the front row of the class so I could see and hear everything. Yes, of course, I was the first one there every morning.

After completing the program and passing the boards, I fractured my left leg, which delayed my choices of departments and choices of placement. I had eight weeks to fantasize about my dream career. I kept looking on the mirror and trying on my nurse uniform with my nurse hat. The revelation, my prophecy, came true, and it was euphoric. After eight weeks for recovery, I had to accept the one area in the hospital I didn't want: the medical floor, which was known as the dungeon, and the night shift at that. I cried. I was told to take it or leave it. During that time, we had three shifts days, evenings, and nights. I said to myself, "There goes my marriage."

Oh yes, how I loved the smell of hospital wards. A smell of rubbing alcohol, that antiseptic smell, the deception of clean. I thought to myself, *Hospitals are probably the biggest germ petri dishes in the world, housed right here.* Although it was a fact, I felt the opposite. To me it was the place we took you in and performed heroics, but there would be only two outcomes. I reported for duty once released to go back to work from my fractured leg. I was given a six-week orientation, and then I was on my own. Many nights, I questioned myself, *Why did I do this?*

As an RN, the buck stopped with me. I perfected my skills and transferred to my dream area of nursing in labor and delivery. I first took the six-week course for competence. I completed the course with a certificate of competence before being allowed to work in that area. I took the in-house course, which was free. Taking an outside course was very expensive. I achieved my dream, but I felt a calling to have more autonomy with my patients. I researched higher options of autonomy. Taking advantage of my education and opportunity, I enrolled in WHNP program in 1996-1998 through San Jose State University.

I myself couldn't believe it was true that you did not need a BSN to enroll. UC Davis had the same program. I did my research. I wanted to take care of my patients and handle their follow-up care. The course was perfect, and this was in my area of expertise. I didn't have to learn the female body because I had one. Nailed it. I have to laugh because the night shift was to be a vengeful punitive move toward me, and I used it to my advantage. It was told to me by a head nurse, "You not never going to get no day shift," with an anonymous witness overhearing it. I tried not to miss a night of work. I was pumped. I started working on my WHNP. Yes, it is true you didn't need your BSN to become a WHNP. I completed the certificate

program in 1998. I said to myself, "I will take my education elsewhere." Soon as I got my WHNP, I began working as WHNP in 1998.

I started working for the famous Dr. Frank O. Brown, an OB-GYN, while doing my internship hours, 950 hours, mind you, without pay. While holding down that "dragon" job, I was laughing all the way to the bank after completing those hours. This job was so gratifying I can't tell you what it did for my self-esteem. Now I was on the payroll. This job as a WHNP made me a great L&D nurse. I was doing vaginal ultrasounds, sizing, and dating. I was doing Pap smears and physical exams as WHNP. I was sizing the pelvis for vaginal delivery, hoping for a 10.5 symmetry, which is not done much anymore. When in labor and problems arise C/S time, never knowing if the vaginal vault was adequate or insufficient for a vaginal delivery. I once asked about this exam during a vaginal exam that was being performed in the clinic at HGH while assisting a CNM. I was told, "Oh, we don't do that anymore." Still craving for more knowledge and searching the best options, I found a program that would suit my needs for more education.

In 1999, I enrolled in Holy Names University to advance my scope of practice and open more options by getting my BSN. I was doing this all while coping with the "dragon" job. Guess what, everybody? I got that BSN and PHN after twenty years of nursing.

Holy Names University

BSN Graduation 2001

I've learned to never let them know what you are thinking; better yet, act oblivious to the fact that you even know that you are being attacked because God has your back. Word to the wise. By now my heart had gotten bigger and so had my brain, I kept going. After graduating with my BSN straight into my master's and FNP program from Holy Names University, I started working as an FNP six months after graduation. I got that job through a church member.

I started working my two days a week in 2003 for the famous Dr. Geoffrey H. Watson. This job is located at the famous historical site in North Oakland. This was Adult Medicine Clinic. I truly believe you need theory behind what you do and why you do it. In addition to that, you also need what is called protocols. They navigate for you the standard of practice and care that is given per institution.

You never decide to reinvent the wheel, it could turn into a bad outcome. Then you have to explain what you did and how you did it. Your goose is cooked if it doesn't fall in line with the protocols for that procedure and institution. I found that a little scary as I was making my exit from the world of nursing that I knew. I have to tell you, I was not about to argue with a novice nurse because the incident would have been based on me being

intimidating in my correction to the novice after the event. Sorry, I don't sweep rugs.

We had started to revert back to the idea that who you liked meant whom the powers would believe in an incident. Not much investigations into matters. I was steady cleaning out my locker, desk, mailbox, and tying up all loose ends. I was on the phone every day with questions concerning my retirement.

I handled calls concerning other people that if I had not been intuitive and able to read between lines, they would have been fired after twenty years of service. For example, "Tell name-less not to come back to work until we contact them." Working in management allowed me to make a management suggestion, such as, "Maybe you should go down to the retirement board and start your paperwork today or wait for their call." I saved several, and myself as well. So much for survival. Too much injustice going on among coworkers and the like. Whatever happened to unanimity?

I believe in the evolution of the cerebral progression. I saw that I was not being promoted. This is why I started racking up the education under the radar. I became a charge nurse for a couple of years, ha. They used to have one on each shift, but

when I was appointed, they had six of them. Everyone was in charge. A couple of years after that, I was appointed Assistant Nurse Manager. For eighteen months, I held this position. Those twelve-hour shifts allowed you a lot of freedom.

There is an old saying, "Never let them see you sweat." I could smell the retirement aroma. I had the years, I had options, and I had the education. You will never guess what happened next. I went in to work on a Saturday morning in September 2009. Even though I was in management, I had to complete my forty hours for the week. That Saturday when I walked out after four hours as usual, something told me to go back and get all your Obama pictures and materials. I did, but I never knew I would never return as an employee. Divine intervention I know it was.

I had been doing hospital SNIF rounds, which I chose my own hours. The job was under the famous Dr. Geoffrey H. Watson. I was working at the James Watson Wellness Center. I knew I was being attacked when I was told that my schedule as an assistant nurse manager, which had been agreed upon when I accepted the position, was being hijacked by several individuals' jealous and evil intentions. This was done by trying to have me work five days a week to block me from my other job opportunity. I

had agreed to do it because I could do patient SNIF hospital rounds at two in the morning if I wanted to. No harm would have been done. The powers that be would have never known I was still making money, until this day. Ha ha to the dumb folks.

Enough of the struggle. I want to tell you how rewarding it truly is to do a job that you love. I looked forward each and every day to come to work and help make a woman's laboring experience nothing short of a wonderful miracle. I always thought that labor and delivery was the happiest ward in the hospital. Each and every birth was unique and special no matter if it was the first or the last birth that woman would ever have. It was exciting to go through the stages of labor with her. The main objective was to have a good outcome. I myself am a mother of two.

This process of a miracle is nothing short of the most exclusive club there is. Every labor or birth, vaginal or not, is different and special. The experience is the human passage into the world. I think of it as a storytelling time. I myself like to tell my daughters what labor was like with each of them. It is something you don't forget.

I would always start with what made me go into the hospital, what time it was, how long their labor was, and all the events until delivery. I remember all the vaginal checks. I used to say to myself, "What are they digging for?" When I became an L&D nurse, I found out. I was able to witness how phenomenal the way a woman's body is equipped to do such a miraculous, mind-blowing and incredible job. Just doing what came natural for a woman's body to do what it is designed to do with little help if there were none.

Now there are always exceptions to the rule. That is where interventions come in. You have pain medication and saddle blocks, which aren't used much anymore. The epidural took the place of that. Sometimes forceps are used. This has become a dying practice. I don't believe this technique is used much by the new generation. The C-section is done for many reasons for the safety of the baby. The main objective is to have a good outcome for everyone involved.

Now we have midwives, doulas, and breast counselors. Some women choose to have home births. I believe I would have tried that, but when I had my first child, pampers were not invented yet. Four years later, the pamper concept had just been invented.

I enjoyed pamper service, lol, and washing and folding my white diapers when I didn't have diaper service. I must say my career as a registered nurse was a dream come true. The work assignment as a nurse was understated. Who would have ever thought a job could be so gratifying to say the least? I thought it would be an ungrateful buyback to retain or preserve my own happiness. Sometimes it's really not always a win-win situation, but in my job position, it was. I do believe that when you start from the bottom, you grow better in what you ultimately want to do. I'll give you an example.

I was first a candy stripper, then became an LVN with an associate's science degree. I worked twenty years raising children, then decided to go for my BSN in 1999. Remember, in 1996, I had gotten my women's health nurse practitioner in the interim. Just walking through doors that only the good Lord can open for us. I keep going until I received a Master's in nursing combined with my FNP. I commanded each department I encountered while an RN at HGH.

This was an advantage I took with pride. Sometimes you were placed or transferred where you were needed for whatever reason. I was able to work in various areas in the hospital. Now that I look back, it makes you a much better practitioner with

all the experiences and being a witness to live cases rather than if you had only read it in textbooks.

Was Almighty setting me up to sit down?

This meaning, as a practitioner, it isn't task oriented. You work through your exams, which dictates your diagnosis. You treat findings with Rx and refer to a specialty. As a nurse, you are on your feet a lot doing concrete evidence tasks and procedures. This is what we do as a nurse, with no autonomy with the patients. We all get older and tire more easily. My heart will always go out to the nurses because we are the patients' first line of defense in the health-care system. Nurses are very intuitive.

I can truly say that the peak of my love affair with nursing was in labor and delivery. It was when I commanded my nursing skills in L&D, like Pitocin introduction to increase contraction, $MgSo_4$ for preeclampsia (hypertension), NSTs for movement of the baby for stress as to how well they can tolerate stress. It is important that the baby must move ten times in one hour. This can also be done at home with documentation while lying on the left side for one hour. I tell you the basic teaching was a thrill for me. Having lack of knowledge is my indicator to dial up the knowledge base.

I remember when I became a scrub nurse. I would like to thank the two nurses who taught me to scrub, Mrs. Vicky Avila and Mrs. Dawn S. Williams. I'd like to give credit where credit is due. I wanted to know how to do everything. I remember when I cried, "Oh, Lord, why did I do this?" Well, by facing my fears head-on, seeking instruction before the buck stops with me. I never felt that way again.

I would like to tell you about the first change throughout the hospital; it was the great computer. There was no more papers. I saw this as a threat. I jump on learning it like white on rice. I wasn't going to be the last one who couldn't operate it. I would like to say that I am an obedient compliant.

I saw images of nurses like this. I believe that nursing is a dedicated, respected profession. I wanted to represent like this. The nurses should wear white uniforms, polished shoes and white shoestrings, white stockings with no runs in them, a navy-blue cape and carrying your nursing hat in a plastic bag to keep it clean and maybe a navy-blue purse.

The unvarying dress code was very attractive to me just like the armed services. It gave me pride and dignity. Slowly over time, the dress code turned dresses into white jeans, with white blouse and white tennis shoes replacing nursing shoes.

By the time I got ready to retire, a person couldn't tell who held what position. I am sorry to say you had more environmental services dressed more like surgeons. Nurses dressed like they were cleaning your house with no name tag on to identify what their job title is, which was often sometimes misunderstood.

Forgive me. I make no apologies, for I have observed. By the time I officially retired in September 22, 2009, after thirty years of service, the preceptorship program was assigned to traveling nurses from other states. They were to teach the standard of care in a specialty area to our novice nurses. The ignorance is a serious liability at hand. Although inexperienced and unqualified as a novice licensed RN with a knowledge deficient due to the lack of training for competence. This is needed to be in the L&D area.

This was how I knew it was time to go. I got images in my mind of those five nurses who wanted to skip the basics and theory of all the nursing theorist to learn in action what they are doing and why. It boggles my mind. I imagine that this type of representation is of the new type of nursing knowledge base. To try this in ICU scares me.

Question to these fine nurses: Who would do this to themselves? They told me to do six months med-surg before transferring to L&D. I did just that and was glad I did. What, no med-surg background? Now they paired you with a traveling nurse, and you did what they taught you, or you did what you saw them do. I call that monkey-see-monkey-do nursing. Most time, your preceptor has gotten monkey-see-monkey-do training in another state.

What was their standards? I say no concrete-base evidence curriculum to follow no notes, no test to take? This is the reason why we have the phrase *standard of care*. Know this, or you lose interpretation, analysis, and clarification of understanding of what you are doing and why. I debated a month or so, Should I make this finale entry? I believe this is the miracle that will help me define my accomplishment as a nurse. Let me proudly tell you about it. It took place on the night shift. We called a C/S, and I was the scrub nurse, which means I handed the instruments to the surgeon.

To define my position is to let nonmedical people understand what I was doing that night in the operating room that very miraculous night. Now as I checked all the positions needed in the room before the incision was made, I noticed something

I had never seen before or heard anyone speak of; it blew my mind. I was making a surveillance or observation of the room. I noticed something so phenomenal. I just could not believe it. This was the perfect exit of my nursing career.

What I observed and witnessed was that every position held in that operating room that night was held by all black professional women, not just women of color but Afro-American women. Wow, that power I felt. The aura in that room. You could hear a pin drop. There was only one explanation.

First, let me tell you what the positions were. We had a surgeon, the assistant surgeon, the anesthesiologist, the scrub nurse (me), the CRNA, the nursery nurse, and the circulating nurse.

The exception was a white male student intern doing his rotation of observation. That person's position was to stand there and observe, no questions. I must say it felt good to see "the shoe on the other foot." I wonder, *Will that anonymous person ever tell that story?*

No apologies, for my belief is a formal education. I believed in science since medicine is not an exact science. We must have synchronism and concrete base evidence and be able to refer

to protocols to back us up. Whatever you envision for yourself, believe it, pursue it, take part in it, and let God open and close your doors. I say to you, dream big, and you won't fall short.

Never let anyone tell you what you cannot do. A nurse must be willing and able to take the pain of injustice, discrimination, being looked over for promotions, and not being acknowledged. Branded, blackballed, despised, envied, even Vu-Doo upon, just to name a few obstacles and hurdles you may have to jump over and go through.

In March 2013, I opened my own Private Practice in adult medicine. A dream bigger that I had ever dreamed, imagined, or could behold. God has a destiny for all of us; you may not see it. I say you better believe it.

THANK YOU TO FLORENCE NIGHTINGALE

IN GOD I TRUST